Endorsements

"As wonderful as contemporary Christian music is to me, I would miss singing the great hymns of the faith. Their words tell the gospel, provide great insight and inspiration, and lift my faith. In this book of devotions, Denise Loock skillfully reflects on some of these hymns by connecting them with Scripture and with our personal spiritual lives. The result is a unique collection of devotions that will touch your heart as you open your hymnal along with your Bible."

Kathleen Hayes
Editor, *The Secret Place*

"Few things are quite so moving, reassuring, and comforting as the familiar texts of inspiring hymns we have loved and sung for generations. Thank you, Denise, for rekindling these messages and shedding new light on songs so near to the hearts of people of faith!"

Dave and Cheryl Ellington
Career Worship Leaders
Covington, KY

"Denise Loock's *Open Your Hymnal* powerfully relates Scripture, hymns, and biblical knowledge to everyday life. Her 30 devotionals are written in such a way that it creates in the reader a desire to reflect upon what has been shared and then to delve deeper. These easy-to-read insights also make the reader want to become familiar with hymns once again and be blessed by their inspired words."

Jane Carrier Allen
Minister of Worship and Bible Professor
Sneads Ferry, NC

"These devotions have poured into my soul a deep love for the God we serve, rooted in the history of biblical and religious figures throughout the ages. What a gift. Denise's style is light but penetrating. It convicts and comforts and draws my heart to the Lord."

Connie Cartisano, Ph.D.
Stay-at-Home Mom and Retreat Speaker
Hackettstown, NJ

"Reaching across all denominations, Denise Loock ties together beloved hymns with their scriptural backgrounds. She brings old-fashioned wording to life by adding a contemporary twist to her devotions. The reader is enlightened, not bewildered, by her inclusion of Greek roots for key words. I would recommend *Open Your Hymnal* to anyone who enjoys singing hymns or wants to give a treasured gift."

Cathy Smith
State Newsletter Editor for United Methodist Women
Ocean, NJ

OPEN YOUR HYMNAL:

Devotions That Harmonize Scripture With Song

OPEN YOUR HYMNAL:
Devotions That Harmonize Scripture With Song

Published by Christian Devotions Ministry,
P. O. Box 6494, Kingsport, TN 37663
ChristianDevotions.us

Published in association with Lighthouse Publishing of the Carolinas.

Available direct from your local bookstore, online, or from the publisher at: christiandevotionsbooks.com

Book Cover and Interior Design by Behind the Gift. Visit us at behindthegift.com

For more info on the author and this book visit:
www.digdeeperdevotions.com/books.aspx

ISBN-13: 978-0-9822065-7-7   ISBN-10: 0-9822065-7-7

Printed in the United States of America.

DEDICATION

To my father and mother,
Donald R. & Dorothy D. Kelso,
who planted a love for God's Word in my heart and
made Psalm 119:105 the cornerstone of our home:

"Your word is a lamp to my feet
and a light for my path."

AUTHOR'S NOTE

s you read the meditations in this book, I encourage you to open your hymnal so that you can access all the lyrics to the songs that are mentioned. You can also find the lyrics to hundreds of songs and hymns online. Three excellent sources are www.cyberhymnal.org, www.songsandhymns.org, and www.hymnsite.com.

TABLE OF CONTENTS

FOREWORD

A hymnal is a treasure-filled volume — the Christian's manual of praise, proclamation, and prayer. When we sing hymns corporately, our individual experience is joined with those around us to become a universal expression of "this we believe." We truly become a part of something bigger than ourselves, and we share in the unity of the body of Christ. To honor the name of God through corporate worship is a Christian's greatest duty and delight.

Some of the hymns mentioned in this book are familiar and have been sung for centuries, some have been neglected, and some have appeared more recently in hymnology. Through witty, insightful, and sometimes poignant writing, Denise draws on the richness of the doctrine and the personal nature of these hymns to encourage us in our Christian faith. Our congregation, sanctuary choir, and I have been blessed beyond measure through Denise's writing. Whether or not hymns are a part of your worship tradition, you will find the timeless truths expressed in these meditations a blessing and encouragement to your soul.

Mark Hahn
Minister of Music
Montgomery Evangelical Free Church
Belle Mead, NJ

INTRODUCTION

In the summer of 2008, I sent a hand-made card to Casey, a friend who was battling a fatal disease. On the front I printed the words of one of my favorite songs, *I Must Tell Jesus*. After Casey received it, she sent me an email and asked if I had written the beautiful poem.

What poem? I wondered. Then I realized she meant the lyrics and that puzzled me. Casey had been a Christian for decades. We had attended the same church for over ten years. The song was in our church hymnal, yet she had never heard it.

I left the computer, walked over to the piano, and picked up a hymnal. As I thumbed through its pages, I recognized songs from childhood that I hadn't sung for years. I also discovered hymns I'd never heard and lyrics that were profoundly rich in biblical truth. I looked at the names of the lyricists. Some I knew—Charles Wesley and Fanny Crosby. Others were strangers to me like Samuel Trevor Francis and William Williams. Who were these hymn writers? What had motivated them to proclaim their faith and pass on their insights in songs?

About that time, I started working in the church office. The minister of music asked me if I would put together the rehearsal schedule and devotion that he distributed to the choir each week. I quickly agreed, realizing that God had given me an opportunity to explore the spiritual heritage of church music and to share my discoveries with others.

Most of the meditations in this collection first appeared in that choir newsletter. I am grateful both to our minister of music and the choir members for their enthusiastic response to my musings. I now open a hymnal with a high regard for the ever-relevant biblical wisdom it contains. May your journey through this book enhance your appreciation for the testimonies of faith and the spiritual truths that shine so brightly on the pages of our hymnals.

Denise K. Loock

SAVING THE DAY – EVERY DAY

ighty Mouse was my favorite cartoon when I was a child. Maybe the little fellow appealed to me because I was small, too. Or maybe I was just mesmerized by the tiny mouse speeding through the air—one arm lifting a runaway train above his head while the other arm steered him past skyscrapers and mountains.

> *For the Mighty One has done great things for me— holy is his name.*
> *Luke 1:49 (NIV)*

Thanks to Mighty Mouse, I just naturally associate the word *mighty* with superhuman strength and miraculous acts of heroism. But in the Bible, *mighty* refers to much more than physical strength.

Hebrew has two words for *mighty*. One is primarily used for heroes and soldiers—*gibbowr*. Israelites would have used that word for Mighty Mouse. The other word, *abiyr*, is used only of God and is translated "Mighty One."

15

Jacob is the first person mentioned in the Bible that called God *Abiyr*, which literally means "the strong." Near the end of his life, as he blessed Joseph, Jacob said, "But his [Joseph's] bow remained steady, his strong arms stayed limber, because of the hand of the Mighty One of Jacob" (Genesis 49:24).

Neither Jacob nor Joseph had been a soldier, so why did Jacob use the word *mighty*? Jacob was not referring to God's physical strength or His military triumphs; he was thinking of God's strength of character—His unchanging nature and His eternal faithfulness. Those were the attributes of God that had sustained Joseph all the years he was separated from his family. And Jacob knew it.

It took Jacob almost all of his 147 years to recognize that both he and his beloved son were totally dependent on God. For most of his life, Jacob had relied on his own cleverness and charisma. Finally, though, he humbly acknowledged that God alone was "The Mighty One," the only reason he and his son Joseph had overcome so many difficulties in their lives.

We often run to our mighty God when enemies tower over us or circumstances threaten to overwhelm us. Yet God's might—his unwavering, rock-solid character—is not just a "here I come to save the day" attribute. God's might is our morning coffee, our lunchtime sandwich, and our evening rest.

English preacher and writer Philip Doddridge wrote the lyrics to *Great God, We Sing Your Mighty Hand* almost 300 years ago. In this classic hymn, he too explores the many ways in which God's might sustains His people

16

every day:

> *By day, by night, at home, abroad,*
> *Still are we guarded by our God.*
> *By his incessant bounty fed,*
> *By His unerring counsel led.*

Take time this week to acknowledge the evidence of God's might in every area of your life—not just the battlegrounds. You can begin with Mary's words in Luke 1:49, "For the Mighty One has done great things for me—holy is his name. His mercy extends to those who fear him, from generation to generation."

♫ *Rest & Reflect*

Think of five everyday ways God demonstrates
His might in your life and then thank
Him for each one.

_____

_____

_____

_____

_____

_____

_____

_____

_____

_____

_____

_____

_____

_____

_____

_____

_____

_____

_____

_____

_____

_____

_____

_____

UNEARNED FAVOR FOR UNDESERVING PEOPLE

Have you ever noticed that Paul began all his letters with a greeting that included the word *grace*? Usually he added the word *peace* and sometimes he included the word *mercy*. Always, however, he highlighted grace.

The word *grace* appears 170 times in the King James Version of the Bible. The first time we read of God's grace is Genesis 6:8: "But Noah found grace in the eyes of the LORD" (KJV). That we can easily understand because Noah was "a righteous man, blameless among the people of his time, and he walked with God" (v. 9).

> *But where sin abounded, grace abounded much more.*
> *Romans 5:20 (NKJV)*

Moses also found grace in God's sight. In Exodus 33 God rewarded Moses' faithful service and humble devotion by allowing him to view His glory in a way no other human being ever had (33:17-23). God told the Israelites, "my servant Moses he is faithful . . . with him

19

I speak face to face" (Numbers 12:7-8).

So where does that leave the rest of us, who haven't built any arks or parted any seas? That's the whole point of grace. It has nothing to do with who we are or what we do. Grace is a gift—the unearned favor of God given to undeserving people like you and me.

Every blessing we receive every day of our lives is a gift of grace. That's the reason Paul begins his epistles with "grace to you." We are justified by grace (Romans 3:24). Spiritual gifts are products of grace (Romans 12:6). The ability to witness is a manifestation of grace (Romans 15:15-16). In 1 Corinthians 3:10 Paul says that God's grace enables him to begin a work and let others finish it. In his next letter, he tells the Corinthians that generosity is a result of grace (2 Corinthians 8:1-7).

No wonder hymn writer John Newton used the adjectives "amazing" and "precious" to describe God's grace. In his classic hymn, he expressed overwhelming gratitude for the unearned favor of God that saves us, teaches us, comforts us, and guides us:

> *'Twas grace that taught my heart to fear,*
> *And grace my fears relieved;*
> *How precious did that grace appear*
> *The hour I first believed.*

> *Through many dangers, toils,*
> *And snares, I have already come;*
> *'Tis grace hath brought me safe thus far,*
> *And grace will lead me home.*

Many American hymnals omit the final two stanzas that Newton wrote, but in them he focuses on the ultimate gift that God's grace made possible—eternal life in heaven:

> *Yes, when this flesh and heart shall fail,*
> *And mortal life shall cease;*
> *I shall possess, within the veil,*
> *A life of joy and peace.*

> *The earth shall soon dissolve like snow,*
> *The sun forebear to shine;*
> *But God, who call'd me here below,*
> *Will be forever mine.*

Someday we will join John Newton, Paul, and the angel choirs in heaven. We will sing praises to the One who enabled us to recognize and receive God's grace and to enjoy forever "a life of joy and peace." Unearned favor for undeserving people that will never end—that's amazing grace.

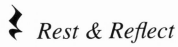 *Rest & Reflect*

*David praised God for many acts of grace
in Psalm 33. What would you add to his list?*

THE SPLENDOR OF HIS LIGHT UNVEILED IN ME

Walter Chalmers Smith, a Scottish pastor, penned the lyrics of *Immortal, Invisible.* He published several volumes of poetry and hymnals during the late 19th century. Originally, the hymn had five stanzas. All of the stanzas make a reference to the glorious light that surrounds God — what is sometimes called the *Shekinah* glory.

> *I am the light of the world. Whoever follows me will never walk in darkness, but will have the light of life.*
> *John 8:12 (NIV)*

Moses witnessed this glory in the desert when he encountered a fire that burned but did not consume the bush. God later made this light visible to the Israelites as the pillar of fire that illuminated their path at night and the cloud that shaded them from the desert heat during the day.

Later, Mount Sinai was enveloped in God's glory "because the LORD descended on it in fire. The smoke billowed up from it like smoke from a furnace, the whole mountain trembled violently, and the sound of the trumpet grew louder and louder" (Exodus 19:18). The Israelites were terrified by this manifestation of God's glory and cried out to Moses, "Speak to us yourself and we will listen. But do not have God speak to us or we will die" (Exodus 20:19).

God honored that request. He spoke only to Moses in a tent "at some distance from the camp" (Exodus 33:7-11). When the Tabernacle was built, He concealed His glory in the Most Holy Place between the cherubim atop the Ark of the Covenant. No one was allowed to enter God's presence except the high priest, and he entered only once a year.

God's glory was veiled by the heavy curtains that blocked the entrance to the Most Holy Place. For centuries, as Smith wrote, God's glory dwelt "in light inaccessible, hid from [human] eyes." Then one day "the true light that gives light to every man" came into the world, and mankind once again witnessed God's glory, "the glory of the one and only," the Lord Jesus Christ (John 1:9,14).

For 33 years the Light of the World walked among us. And then when He died on the Cross, the veil in the Most Holy Place was torn in half—God's glory would no longer have to be hidden from us.

In the original fourth stanza of Smith's hymn, he included the following prayer:

> *But of all Thy rich graces*
> *This grace Lord impart*
> *Take the veil from our faces,*
> *The vile from our heart.*

Although the wording is a little old-fashioned, we certainly can understand Smith's intent. He was referring to Paul's words in 2 Corinthians 3:16—"whenever anyone turns to the Lord, the veil is taken away." What an incredible privilege we are given—not only are our sins forgiven, but we also gain access to the presence of God. Both the "veil" and the "vile" are gone.

Furthermore, Paul says that we who now have "unveiled faces" actually reflect God's *Shekinah* glory because the Holy Spirit lives in each of us (v. 17-18). With renewed awe and gratitude may we sing:

> *Most blessed, most glorious,*
> *The Ancient of Days,*
> *Almighty, victorious—*
> *Thy great Name we praise.*

♪ *Rest & Reflect*

How brightly does God's glory shine through you? Can those around you see that you are "being transformed into His likeness with ever-increasing glory" (2 Corinthians 3:18)?

What Verse Does My Life Display?

I've never seen John 3:17 painted on a barn, emblazoned on a t-shirt, or displayed at a sporting event. Nevertheless, verse 17 is just as crucial to the Gospel as verse 16 is. Why? Verse 17 clarifies the meaning of verse 16. Like a flashing red light it exclaims, "Attention: Don't miss the point of the previous verse!"

> *For God did not send his son into the world to condemn the world, but to save the world through him.*
>
> *John 3:17 (NIV)*

What is the point of John 3:16? The gift of salvation is the outgrowth of God's unconditional and inexplicable love for mankind. John 3:16 is a love letter. That's the reason verse 17 says, "God did not send his son into the world to condemn the world."

The Greek word translated "condemn" is *krino*, which means "to inflict a penalty." In other words, punishing people was not Jesus' objective when He came to earth 2,000 years ago. What was His purpose? Verse 17 tells us that, too—"to save the world."

How was that going to happen? Jesus described His ministry when He taught in the temple. Quoting Isaiah, He said that He had come to "preach good news to the poor, proclaim freedom for the prisoners, and release the oppressed" (Luke 4:18). Later, the picture Jesus used for His rescue mission was a hen gathering her chicks (Luke 13:34).

He told the disciples to "do good" to their enemies."Do not condemn," He cautioned, but forgive and be merciful (Luke 6:35-37). In the upper room before His betrayal He said, "By this shall all men know that you are my disciples, if you love one another" (John 13:35).

Sharing the message of salvation should be an act of love. Before I adhere a John 3:16 bumper sticker to my car or tattoo the reference on my forearm, I should think about how consistently I manifest God's love to those around me. What do my Christian brothers and sisters hear when I disagree with them? How do I respond to my obnoxious neighbor when he criticizes my children? What faces do I make when a customer at the grocery store wheels a cartload of items into the express lane?

When John Stainer composed the music to *God So Loved the World*, he used the words of John 3:16-17 as his lyrics. In the song, he repeats "God so loved the world" once at the beginning and three times at the end. The echo of the phrase as the song ends effectively emphasizes the theme of the two Scripture verses—God's astounding love for us:

God so loved the world,
God so loved the world,
that He gave His only begotten Son,
that whoso believeth, believeth in Him
should not perish, should not perish
but have everlasting life, everlasting life,
everlasting, everlasting life,
God so loved the world,
God so loved the world,
God so loved the world.

God did not send His Son into the world to condemn us but to redeem us. The love that made salvation possible is also the love God asks us to reflect through our words and deeds. 1 John 4:11 says, "Dear friends, since God so loved us, we ought also to love one another." May that be the verse we display on our faces and paint on the walls of our lives.

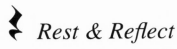 *Rest & Reflect*

Read Ephesians 4:29-32.
How can you display God's love to others today
through your words and actions?

JESUS, THE GREAT SHEPHERD

" "The Good Shepherd" is one of the most endearing names that Jesus bears. But did you know that Jesus is also called "The Great Shepherd"?

Each of these adjectives reflects a different aspect of Jesus' ministry. He told the crowd in John 10 that as the Good Shepherd He came to protect His sheep from robbers and hired hands who were more interested in their own well-being than in the safety of the sheep. He declared in verses 11 and 15 that He would voluntarily sacrifice His life for the sheep. That was the objective of His earthly ministry.

> *"Being confident of this, that He who began a good work in you will carry it on to completion until the day of Jesus Christ"*
> *Philippians 1:6 (NIV)*

But now Jesus sits at the right hand of God the Father in the heavenly realms and He bears a slightly different name—the Great Shepherd:

"May the God of peace, who through the blood of the eternal covenant brought back from the dead our Lord Jesus, that *great shepherd* of the sheep, equip you with everything good for doing his will and may he work in us what is pleasing to him, through Jesus Christ, to whom be glory for ever and ever" (Hebrews 13:20-21, author's italics).

In these verses, the writer of Hebrews is emphasizing Jesus' present ministry as the "finisher of our faith" (Hebrews 12:1). The NIV translators use the word "equip," but "made perfect" and "made complete" are more accurate translations of the Greek word *katartizo*.

One of the marvels of our salvation is the truth that God is not finished with us. He redeemed us, yes, but now He is sanctifying us—remaking us into the likeness of His Son. Hebrews 13:20-21 declares that God completes this work through the power of Jesus Christ, our Great Shepherd. The writer also says, "The Lord disciplines those he loves" (12:6), and "the Lord is my helper; I will not be afraid. What can man do to me?"(13:4)

The hymn, *Savior Like a Shepherd Lead Us*, highlights Jesus' finishing work, too. The lyrics, attributed to Dorothy A. Thrupp, echo the truths conveyed in Hebrews about the ministry of our Great Shepherd who leads us, feeds us, and guards us:

Savior, like a Shepherd lead us,
Much we need thy tender care;
In thy pleasant pastures feed us;
For our use Thy folds prepare.

We are thine; do Thou befriend us:
Be the guardian of our way:
Keep Thy flock; from sin defend us:
Seek us when we go astray.

Thrupp also recognized that the "tender care" our Shepherd provides should motivate us to obey. She wrote, "Early let us seek Thy favor; early let us do Thy will." How else could we possibly respond to our Shepherd, who loved us enough to redeem us and continues to love us enough to care for us every day in every way?

♫ *Rest & Reflect*

What kind of sheep are you? Do you follow your Great Shepherd with a willing or a wayward heart?

EVEN WHEN I CAN'T SEE YOU

than the Ezrahite was feeling frazzled. He was one of the temple musicians, but his world was collapsing around him and he didn't feel like singing. Instead he poured out his heart in a song. We call it Psalm 89.

Some Bible scholars believe Ethan was living through the disintegration of Solomon's kingdom when the ten northern tribes crowned Jeroboam and the two southern tribes crowned Rehoboam. Other scholars date the psalm much later, during the years just before the Babylonian captivity.

> *O LORD God Almighty, who is like you?*
> *You are mighty, O Lord, and your faithfulness surrounds you.*
> **Psalm 89:8** (NIV)

When Ethan wrote the psalm doesn't matter as much as *why* he wrote it. God had told David, "Your house and your kingdom will endure forever" (2 Samuel 7:16). As Ethan witnessed the ruin of the Davidic kingdom, he wondered what had happened to the "forever" in God's promise:

35

> You have exalted the right hand of his foes;
> You have made his enemies rejoice.
> You have turned back the edge of his sword
> And have not supported him in battle.
> You have put an end to his splendor
> And cast his throne to the ground.
> You have cut short the days of his youth;
> You have covered him with a mantle of shame.
> (Psalm 89:42-45)

Those words sound a lot more like betrayal than faithfulness, a lot more like hatred than love. Nevertheless, at the beginning of Psalm 89 Ethan praised the very attributes he later claimed were missing. In verses one and two he said,

> I will sing of the Lord's great love forever;
> With my mouth I will make your faithfulness
> Known through all generations.
> I will declare that your love stands firm forever,
> That you established your faithfulness
> in heaven itself.

How could Ethan praise God's faithfulness and love in verses 1-37 and then mourn their loss in verses 38-51? The answer is profound: What Ethan saw did not alter what he knew. In other words, his intellect, not his emotions, fueled his faith. Even though he wanted to see the evidence of God's faithfulness while he was still alive and mourned the destruction around him, he still believed in the certainty of restoration. He relied on God's faithfulness.

We all feel like Ethan sometimes. We want to see the

fulfillment of God's promises. However, faith requires more of us. Hebrews 11:39 says, "These were all commended for their faith, yet none of them received what had been promised."

The "forever" of God's character is the foundation of genuine faith. He never changes. Therefore, like Ethan, we can be sure that God will fulfill every one of His promises even when we see no evidence of it.

Horatio G. Spafford wrote the lyrics to *It Is Well with My Soul* after the tragic deaths of his children. Like Ethan, Spafford continued to praise God because he counted on God's faithfulness:

> *When peace, like a river, attendeth my way,*
> *When sorrows like sea billows roll—*
> *Whatever my lot, Thou hast taught me to say,*
> *It is well, it is well with my soul.*

When we focus on God's unchanging nature, we too can sing "it is well with my soul" because the clouds of inexplicable circumstances will one day dissipate and our "faith will be sight. Praise the Lord, praise the Lord, O my soul."

 *Rest & Reflect*

Are you longing for God to fulfill a promise or answer a prayer? What aspects of His character can you focus on as you wait?

KEEPING THE CROSS IN CHRISTMAS

Flipping through the Christmas CDs at Barnes and Nobles one day, I wondered why so many artists put *What Child Is This?* on their holiday albums—everyone from Johnny Mathis to Jessica Simpson along with numerous Christian soloists and groups.

My musical husband suggested that the carol was a popular choice because its simple melody falls within most voice ranges. No high notes like *O Holy Night*, no low notes like *Sweet Little Jesus Boy*. His answer made sense, but since I couldn't remember the carol's lyrics I decided to do a little investigating at home.

> **Today in the town of David a Savior has been born to you; He is Christ the Lord.**
> **Luke 2:11 (NIV)**

William C. Dix wrote *What Child Is This?* The lyrics are based on one of his poems, *The Manger Throne*. As I read the carol's original words, I noticed that modern versions use the end of the first stanza as the song's refrain:

39

This, this is Christ the King,
Whom shepherds guard and angels sing;
Haste, haste to bring him laud,
The Babe, the Son of Mary.

The second stanza intrigued me because it emphasized the purpose of Christ's birth so graphically:

Why lies He in such mean estate,
Where ox and ass are feeding?
Good Christians, fear, for sinners here
The Silent Word is pleading.
Nails, spear shall pierce Him through,
The cross be borne for me, for you.
Hail, Hail the Word made flesh,
The Babe, the Son of Mary.

None of the artists or groups who recorded this song used these lyrics. Not even hymnals include them. Why not? Granted, the lyrics are not very merry, but omitting the theological significance of Christmas reduces it to nothing more than an elaborate Hallmark® birth announcement. And that is not a biblical perspective at all.

The Bible consistently links the joyous birth of Christ to the somber truth of His death. The angel told Joseph to name the child Jesus because He would save His people from their sins (Matthew 1:21). The heavenly host proclaimed, "a Savior has been born" (Luke 2:11). And the magi brought myrrh, a resin used in embalming

40

mixtures.

William Dix grasped the importance of connecting the celebration of Christ's birth with the inevitability of His death. To view Jesus simply as a babe in a manger is spiritually dangerous. It makes it too easy to leave Him in the stable — a poignant character in a sentimental holiday story.

Editing the cross out of our Christmas carols is also perilous. It distances us from the convicting truth that the wooden manger would become a wooden cross, the swaddling clothes a purple robe, and the adoring shepherds a jeering mob.

The Son of Mary was the Son of God who became the Son of Man and gave his life as a ransom for many (Mark 10:45). Let's do more than keep Christ in Christmas. Let's keep the cross in Christmas, too.

Rest & Reflect

Read Luke 2:8-14.
Note all the things the angels say about Jesus. How can
you present a well-rounded portrait of Jesus to those you
encounter?

RESTORING OUR FELLOWSHIP WITH GOD

God has always desired the companionship of those He created in His image. In the beginning He initiated the daily times of fellowship with Adam and Eve. Then He sought them out even when He knew they had sinned and opened a chasm of unrighteousness between His holiness and their imperfection.

> *The virgin will be with child and will give birth to a son, and they will call him Immanuel—which means, "God with us."*
> *Matthew 1:23 (NIV)*

Hundreds of years later, when God delivered the Israelites from Egypt, He declared that they were "his treasured possession" (Exodus 19:5). He told Moses to "make a sanctuary" so that He could "dwell" among His people (Exodus 25:8).

But before God had even finished giving Moses the blueprints for the Tabernacle, the Israelites had created a golden calf and had begun to worship it. And although

God repeatedly wooed them and disciplined them, they never fully abandoned the pagan practices they had adopted in Egypt.

The God whose splendor and holiness was hidden behind the thick curtains of the Most Holy Place frightened them. They wanted a god they could see, a god they could touch, a god they could understand. God mourned over their fickle, foolish faithlessness, yet He understood their need. He had always intended to provide a God they could see.

Therefore on a quiet night near a small village, a tattered group of shepherds heard the divine proclamation for which the souls of all mankind yearned: "Today in the town of David a Savior has been born to you; he is Christ the Lord" (Luke 2:11). Born into the world of men was the Lord of the universe. God "became flesh and made his dwelling among us" (John 1:14).

The miracle of Bethlehem is not that Jesus *could* come to earth but that He *chose* to come. He volunteered to leave the holy splendor of heaven and the perfect fellowship of God the Father and the Holy Spirit. The Incarnation is the official manifesto of God's unchanging, never-ending desire to commune with those He created and loves. That astounds me. It humbles me. And it convicts me.

The writer of *O Come, O Come Emmanuel* conveys that same emotional mixture in his classic Christmas carol. He rejoiced in the fulfillment of God's promise to provide a redeemer and restore our fellowship with Him:

> *O come, O come, Emmanuel,*
> *And ransom captive Israel*
> *That mourns in lonely exile here*
> *Until the Son of God appear.*

> *O come, O come, O Bright and Morning Star,*
> *And bring us comfort from afar*
> *Dispel the shadows of the night*
> *And turn our darkness into light.*

But he also prayed, "To us the path of knowledge show, And cause us in her way to go." Our Savior's advent should fill our hearts with joy, but it should also motivate us to obey Him so that we can enjoy His companionship.

The lyrics of *O Come, O Come Emmanuel* also refer to the day when the Key of David, Jesus Christ, will "open wide our heavenly home" (Revelation 3:7). On that day our relationship with God will be as pure and complete as the relationship He shared with Adam and Eve in Eden. God's original purpose fulfilled—His joy and ours complete. What a glorious day that will be.

♪ *Rest & Reflect*

*Jesus came to earth to restore our fellowship with Him.
What do you do each day to preserve and improve your
relationship with Him?*

_____

_____

_____

_____

_____

_____

_____

_____

_____

_____

_____

_____

_____

_____

_____

_____

_____

_____

_____

_____

_____

WORSHIP THE KING OF KINGS

"Where is he that is born the king of the Jews?" How ironic that the first people to acknowledge Jesus' royalty were a travel-worn group of Gentile astrologers who had seen a dazzling star in the heavens. The star's uniqueness convinced them that a king had been born. Its brilliance compelled them to discover the child's identity.

> *On his robe and on his thigh he has this name written:*
> *KING OF KINGS*
> *AND LORD*
> *OF LORDS.*
> *Revelation 19:16 (NIV)*

When the Magi arrived at the lowly home of Mary and Joseph, the whole village must have gawked at the procession. The entourage would have been impressive, not merely three men as the Christmas carol suggests — but probably dozens of people, including servants that had cared for the astrologer-priests, their animals, and their provisions as they traveled.

47

I envision the crowd pressing around the house straining to hear and see what the travelers were doing, what they were saying. The visit must have been the gossip topic at the village well and in the marketplace. Who were these travelers and why had they come to visit Joseph, the carpenter?

But when Mary and Joseph fled to Egypt, the wonder of the Magi's visit evaporated. When the couple returned to Nazareth many months later, no one seemed to remember anything special about Joseph's family.

The crowd's fascination faded, but Mary pondered these things in her heart (Luke 2:19). How often did she and Joseph talk about the events surrounding Jesus' birth? How often did they reflect on the angel's words: "the Lord God will give him the throne of his father David, and he will reign over the house of Jacob forever; his kingdom will never end" (Luke 1:32-33)? How often did they open the precious containers of gold, frankincense, and myrrh—regal gifts for a royal child?

And decades later, what did Mary think when she saw the inscription Pilate had written, hanging above her son's bleeding and broken body: "This is Jesus, the King of the Jews"? Did she reflect on the words of the angel who had so joyously announced that she would bear the Messiah, David's royal heir? Did she think about the Magi paying homage on bended knee to her son? Or was she simply too overwhelmed with grief to focus on anything but the chill of death and the horror of crucifixion?

What contrast could be more dramatic than the one between the Magi's visit and the scene at the cross? Yet both images convey the truth of Jesus' true identity, "the King of the Jews."

When we sing *O Worship the King*, we should be mindful of both portraits—the adoration of the Magi and the ridicule of the crowd at the cross. Jesus' birth and his death equally manifest "his wonderful love for us." Today He is "pavilioned in splendor and girded with praise" as He sits at the right hand of God the Father because He was willing to become both the newborn king and the redeeming king. May we always be quick to lift our praise to Jesus, the King of Kings:

> *O worship the King all glorious above,*
> *And gratefully sing His wonderful love;*
> *Our Shield and Defender, the Ancient of Days,*
> *Pavilioned in splendor and girded with praise.*

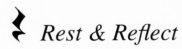

Rest & Reflect

How often do you praise the King of Kings?
Read David's list of praises in Psalm 145.
Then add a few of your own.

THE PRIVILEGE OF PRAISE

As the overseas missions director of an international Christian organization, my father traveled all over the world. He saw some of the most beautiful, breath-stopping places on earth. One of the sights that thrilled him most was the night sky over the plains of Kenya. For him, the brilliance of the stars and the vastness of their dark velvet backdrop was an unforgettable manifestation of God's glory and his own insignificance.

> *What is man that you are mindful of him, the son of man that you care for him?*
> *Psalm 8:4 (NIV)*

Every time I read Psalm 8 I am reminded of my father's experience in Kenya. Most scholars agree that David's words in verse 3 are a reference to the hundreds of evenings he spent on the Judean hillsides shepherding his father's flocks.

51

The sky's grandeur overwhelmed him for two reasons: It proved how immensely powerful God was and emphasized how powerless he was. However, this did not frighten David. It exhilarated him.

In his commentary on Psalm 8 Dr. James Boice noted, "it is certain that nothing under the heavens can praise God adequately. Yet this is what men and women have the privilege of doing." And the privilege of praising God gives human beings "a significance and honor above everything else God has created."*

This privilege of bringing God glory awed David. And every human being shares that honor equally. David highlighted children and infants in Psalm 8:2, but I think of other groups as well—the disabled, the elderly, and the invalids. In the nursing home or in the corporate office, changing diapers or changing international policies, preparing a sermon or preparing a meal—at any age, at any time, in any place, we can bring God glory by praising Him.

Psalm 8 begins and ends with the matchless majesty of God. In the middle, David pauses to reflect on his own uniqueness. As David says in verse 5, we have been "crowned . . . with glory and honor," uniquely suited to respond to God in a way no other creation can.

No wonder so many hymnists, from Isaac Watts in *We Sing the Greatness of Our God* to Stuart Hine in *How Great Thou Art* have been inspired by Psalm 8. Watts observed:

We sing the goodness of the Lord
That filled the earth with food;
He formed the creatures with His word
And then pronounced them good.
Lord, how Thy wonders are displayed
Where'er we turn our eyes
In every season of the year,
And through the changing skies.

There's not a plant or flower below
But makes Thy glories known;
And clouds arise and tempests blow
By order from Thy throne,
While all that borrows life from Thee
Is ever in Thy care,
And everywhere that man can be,
Thou, God, art present there.

When we consider the majesty of God's handiwork and the privilege we have of proclaiming His glory, how could we not sing of His greatness?

*James M. Boice, *Psalms: An Expositional Commentary*. Volume 1. Grand Rapids: Baker Books, 1994, p.68-69.

 *Rest & Reflect*

Take time to notice the wonders of God's natural world today. Then thank Him for the care He provides for every individual thing He created.

SINGING A LAMENT OF PRAISE

ometimes I don't feel like singing a song of praise. In fact, on some days the sound of a joyful song of thanksgiving can be as irritating as the whine of a dentist's drill. When the piercing sword of an inexplicable illness, a family crisis, or a spiritual ambush flattens me or someone I love, raising a loud anthem of heartfelt praise seems emotionally impossible.

In these valleys of bewilderment and pain, I head for the psalms—not the laughing, exultant psalms like Psalm 8,

> *How can we sing the songs of the LORD while in a foreign land?*
>
> *Psalm 137:4 (NIV)*

but the weeping, mournful psalms like Psalm 137. Psalm 137 is a lament—a "formal expression of sorrow or mourning; an elegy or dirge." The first verse conveys the depth of sorrow that the Jewish captives experienced as they were dragged off to Babylon: "By the rivers of Babylon we sat and wept when we remembered Zion."

Few of us will ever know the horror of a war-ravaged

55

environment—cities burned, loved ones raped and murdered, conquerors gloating over our humiliation. No wonder the captives laid their harps aside (v. 2). No wonder the psalmist asked, "How can we sing the songs of the Lord while in a foreign land?"(v. 4)

And yet, the wonder of Psalm 137 is that even in the morass of his misery, the psalmist declares his faith in God—he will not forget Jerusalem, he will not forget his inheritance, he will not forget God's vow to exalt his people and crush their enemies (v.6). Therefore, his lament becomes a testimony of praise.

I Must Tell Jesus, written by Elisha A. Hoffman, is also a lament of praise. In it, Hoffman pours out his grief to the Savior who "always loves and cares for his own." The repetition in the refrain emphasizes both the urgency of Hoffman's need and the certainty of the solution:

> *I must tell Jesus! I must tell Jesus!*
> *I cannot bear my burdens alone;*
> *I must tell Jesus! I must tell Jesus!*
> *Jesus can help me, Jesus alone.*

Isaiah put it this way: God alone is able to "comfort all who mourn, and provide for those who grieve in Zion—to bestow upon them a crown of beauty instead of ashes, the oil of gladness instead of mourning, and a garment of praise instead of a spirit of despair" (61:2-3).

There will always be times in our lives when, like the Babylonian exiles, we sit by the waters and weep—days when the crown of "glory and honor" David speaks of in Psalm 8 feels more like a crown of thorns. But our lament can still glorify God's name if we, like the writer of Psalm 137, reflect on the faithfulness of His promises. And who knows? To the One who will someday wipe away all our tears, our lament of faith may be sweeter music than the most joyful song of praise.

♪ *Rest & Reflect*

Read David's lament of praise in Psalm 13. Then write or pray your own lament of praise and place your burdens in Jesus' hands.

THE DIVINE WHISPERER

I doubt that anyone has ever used the words "softly and tenderly" to describe the sound of my voice. In elementary school, I was often reprimanded for talking too loudly and too often. When I became a teacher, people complained that they could hear my voice down the hall and through the walls. Somehow, I have never managed to fine-tune my indoor voice.

I am somewhat comforted by the fact that Jesus didn't always speak softly and tenderly either. Matthew 23 records his scalding condemnation of the scribes and Pharisees—the "whitewashed tombs . . . woe to you . . . full of hypocrisy and wickedness" lecture he gave them.

Praise the Lord, O my soul, and forget not all his benefits.
Psalm 103:2 (NIV)

Ironically, though, Matthew 23 ends with a verse I have always associated with the "softly and tenderly" Jesus: "O Jerusalem, Jerusalem, you who kill the prophets and stone those sent to you, how often I have longed to gather your children together, as a hen gathers her chicks under her wings, but you were not willing" (v. 37).

59

This verse is an odd mixture of compassion and condemnation—the nurturing image of a mother hen conflicting with the violence of Jerusalem's citizens. Jesus is clearly grieving over the people's willful rejection of their rightful king and the spiritual blindness that would lead to their eternal condemnation. Many scholars suggest that Jesus is also mourning the destruction that was coming soon at the hands of the Romans in 70 A. D., and the suffering that would follow for many generations until He returns in power and glory.

Sometimes we piously shake our heads in dismay over the Jews' failure to embrace Jesus, and yet we, too, grieve His heart when we value other things and other people more highly than we value our relationship with Him.

In *Softly and Tenderly* William Thompson asks two questions that apply to Christians just as much as they apply to skeptics:

Why should we linger when Jesus is pleading,
Pleading for you and for me?
Why should we wait, then, and heed not His mercies,
Mercies for you and for me?

Both the Hebrew and Greek words for "mercy" refer to much more than the forgiveness of sins. They are general terms that encompass God's goodness, kindness, and favor in every area of our lives.

In Psalm 103:2, David admonishes himself, saying, "forget not all his benefits." He then lists numerous ways God blesses him every day: Forgiveness and healing, love and compassion, satisfaction and renewal. These daily blessings are God's soft and tender voice that we often ignore.

I recently wrote this verse across the top of my daily prayer list: "Every day I will praise you" (Psalm 145:2). I want eyes that recognize God's gifts and ears that hear God's indoor voice. Don't you?

♩ *Rest & Reflect*

Think back over the events of the last few days.
Has God been speaking to you in His indoor or His outdoor
voice? What has He been saying? Are you listening?

_____

_____

_____

_____

_____

_____

_____

_____

_____

_____

_____

_____

_____

_____

_____

_____

_____

_____

_____

_____

_____

_____

THE GLORY DUE HIS NAME

he procession was impressive. Hundreds of Levites, musicians, singers, and worshippers accompanied the king as he traveled from the house of Obed-Edom to Jerusalem. In fact, 1 Chronicles 15:28 states that "all Israel" participated in this event "with shouts, with the sounding of rams' horns and trumpets, and of cymbals, and the playing of lyres and harps."

But as for me, I will always proclaim what God has done, I will sing praise to the God of Jacob. Psalm 75:9 (NLT)

What was the occasion? A coronation? Victory over the Philistines? The birth of the king's son? No. The Ark of the Covenant was being transported to its new home.

In the midst of this joyous celebration David "committed to Asaph and his associates [a] psalm of thanks to the LORD" (1 Chronicles 16:7). The psalm is a jubilant tribute to

God, and in it David uses the phrase "Ascribe to the LORD the glory due his name" (16:29).

David and his subjects sang and danced all the way to Jerusalem because they were celebrating what God had done in Israel—He had established peace, He had given them victory over their enemies, and they had a king who ruled wisely and well. David was also honoring Israel's history—God's covenant with Abraham, Isaac, and Jacob and the land inheritance that their descendents enjoyed (vv. 16-22).

One interesting aspect of this psalm is that even though it is sung by Israelites, David wanted it to be heard by "the nations" (16:8). I wonder how many Gentile spectators stood along the roadside and marveled at the exuberant procession David led that day. Did any of them mock him, as his wife Michal did? When David returned home, she called him a "vulgar fellow" (2 Samuel 6:20). David rebuked her and said, "I will celebrate before the Lord," and he didn't care if others considered that humiliating and undignified (v. 21-22).

Johann J. Schutz expressed a similar sentiment in *Sing Praise to God Who Reigns Above*. Like David, he wanted both Christians and skeptics to witness his exuberant joy. Schutz supported German Pietism, a 17th century Lutheran revivalist movement that sought to reignite the spiritual fervor Martin Luther had inspired in the 16th century. In the fourth stanza of his best-known hymn Schutz wrote:

> *That all my gladsome way along,*
> *I sing aloud His praises,*
> *That men may hear the grateful song*
> *My voice unwearied raises.*

Gathering with other Christians on a Sunday morning and singing praises to our God certainly glorifies His name. But like David and Schutz, we should also want to "make known among the nations what he has done" (1 Chronicles 16:8). Therefore, those who see us the rest of the week should also hear us "tell of all His wonderful acts" (16:9). In that way, we will truly proclaim "the glory due His name."

 *Rest & Reflect*

Have you spoken of "God's wonderful acts" recently?
What is your "grateful song"?
Who could you share it with today?

WHAT'S IN A NAME?

My husband and I tossed a lot of choices in the rejection pile when we were selecting names for our first child. We had both been teachers for many years, and certain names awakened negative memories. Others were just too common. We refused to add another "John" or "Mary" to a fellow teacher's roster.

> *"At the name of Jesus every knee should bow, in heaven and on earth and under the earth, and every tongue confess that Jesus Christ is Lord to the glory of God the Father."*
> *Philippians 2:10-11 (NIV)*

Shakespeare's Juliet said, "What's in a name? . . . a rose by any other name would smell as sweet." But everyone knows that some names drag stinky baggage behind them. For example, my husband and I never considered naming our son Judas, Samson, or Napoleon. We also omitted Delilah, Jezebel, and Cleopatra from the list of girls' names.

67

Other names reek with ridicule. I admire C. S. Lewis, but I wasn't tempted to name my son Clive. I am also an original *Star Trek* fan, but I wasn't going to burden my daughter with the name Uhura.

In the Bible, names often have spiritual significance. People may have snickered when Abram, "exalted father," revealed that he had no children. But God knew better and changed his name to Abraham, "father of a multitude." The apostle Paul also had a name change. Saul means "desired," but Paul means "small or little." (Maybe the former Pharisee needed a continual reality check).

When the angel appeared to Joseph of Nazareth, he told the expectant father to name his son Jesus, "for he will save his people from their sins" (Matthew 1:21). *Jesus* is the Greek form of the Hebrew word *Yehowshuwa* which means "Jehovah is salvation."

It intrigues me that in the gospel accounts, most individuals called Jesus "Teacher"—a title of respect, but not necessarily an indication of devotion. Ironically, that is still the name by which most people know Jesus. The skeptics I know, as well as the ones I hear speaking publicly, quickly identify Jesus as a teacher—at least in the sense that his instruction was wise and worthy of emulation. Sadly, however, they reject him as "salvation."

In *The Trouble with Jesus*, Joe Stowell observed, "A one-size-fits-all Jesus must be tolerant of everyone, judgmental toward none, kind but not analytical, loving but not disciplining . . . a bland, almost boring, toothless, inoffensive, non-divisive, disposable Jesus."* And that is not the biblical Jesus at all. Jesus said, "I am *the* way,

68

the truth, and *the* life " (John 14:6, author's italics). No wiggle-room there. Peter said, "Salvation is found in *no one else*" (Acts 4:12, author's italics). No alternative routes there, either.

In *Blessed Be the Name* W. H. Clark wrote:

> *His name above all names shall stand,*
> *Exalted more and more,*
> *At God the Father's own right hand,*
> *Where angel-hosts adore.*

Truly, no other name signifies so much to so many— forgiveness and salvation, grace and new life, hope and a heavenly home. Jesus. *Salvation*. Name above all names. May we always speak that blessed name with reverence.

*Joseph M Stowell. *The Trouble with Jesus*, Chicago: Moody Publishers, 2003, p.80.

♩ *Rest & Reflect*

What does the name Jesus mean to you?
How do others know that His name is precious to you?

ENGRAVED ON THE PALMS OF GOD'S HANDS

When I was in the third grade, our teacher, Miss Richards, gave each of her students a package of five pencils for Christmas. Engraved on each pencil in shiny gold letters were our first and last names. I remember sliding my thumb across the surface of a pencil and relishing the unique texture of my name.

> *No one can snatch them out of my Father's hand.*
> *John 10:29 (NIV)*

Maybe Miss Richards simply wanted to keep a more accurate record of whose pencils were rolling around on the classroom floor or which absent-minded student left his pencil in the sharpener. No matter what her motives were, for us the gift represented something every human being values — the pride of ownership. We also learned that ownership cultivated both responsibility

71

and accountability. No longer could any of us use the excuse, "It's not my pencil."

I am reminded of those pencils when I read Isaiah 49. Isaiah ministered to God's people during a devastating historical period. The inhabitants of the northern tribes and of Samaria had been conquered by Assyria. Sennacherib's army was terrorizing the people who lived in Judah. In Isaiah 49:14 the people lament, "The LORD has forsaken me, the LORD has forgotten me."

But Isaiah assured the southern tribes that God had not forsaken them. In fact, God could not forget them any more than a mother can forget about the child she is nursing. In verse 16 God said to His people, "See I have engraved you on the palms of my hands: your walls are ever before me."

In this comforting message, God reviewed what His people should have known — "I will never break my covenant with you" (Judges 2:1). When He said, "your walls are ever before me," He was acknowledging the devastation of His people, but He was also promising that the walls of Jerusalem would be repaired when the exiles eventually returned to Palestine.

Later in chapter 49 the LORD said, "those who hope in me will not be disappointed" (v. 23). The people of Jerusalem were certainly sorrowful at that time, but they could still count on God to uphold His covenantal promises.

When life's circumstances pummel us, we may also feel as though God has forgotten us, but He has not. He has engraved our names on the palms of His hands, too, and our brokenness is ever before Him. He rubs His thumb along the unique texture of our names and says,

"This one is mine. I know him. I know her. I take full responsibility for my beloved child's well-being."

Maybe George Wade Robinson was thinking of Isaiah 49:16 when he wrote *I Am His, and He Is Mine*. The simplicity of the melody and the confidence of the lyrics both underscore the song's bedrock truth—God's love for His children is eternal and His ownership irrefutable:

> *Loved with everlasting love,*
> *Led by grace that love to know;*
> *Gracious Spirit from above,*
> *Thou hast taught me it is so!*
> *O this full and perfect peace!*
> *O this transport all divine!*
> *In a love which cannot cease,*
> *I am His, and He is mine.*

If you're feeling forgotten this week, look at the palm of your hand and remind yourself that you are secure in God's care. "His forever, only His," wrote Robinson. We can experience "full and perfect peace" because we are engraved on the palms of God's hands.

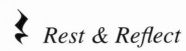 *Rest & Reflect*

Read God's message of comfort in Jeremiah 31:2-5.
Claim those promises as your own and praise God for His
everlasting love.

THE CALL TO HEAR . . . AND OBEY

large crowd had gathered on the banks of the Jordan River. Many came simply to gawk at the camel-coated, locust-eating Nazarite named John. A few came to hear his call for repentance. Many watched as a stranger with noble bearing waded into the water to be baptized.

None of them were prepared for what happened next. The heavens opened and a thunderous voice proclaimed, "This is my beloved Son in whom I am well-pleased" (Matthew 3:17 KJV). The crowd trembled in fear and amazement.

> *Jesus replied, If anyone loves me, he will obey my teaching.*
> *John 14:23 (NIV)*

Three years later a small group of men stood on a high mountain—Jesus and his closest friends, Peter, James, and John. Suddenly, the skies parted again and a luminous cloud descended: "This is my beloved Son in whom I am well-pleased." Jesus himself was clothed in light so dazzling that the disciples fell to the ground in fear and amazement.

On these two occasions, at the beginning and the end of Jesus' earthly ministry, God the Father spoke from the throne of heaven identifying His Son and announcing His approval of His Son's mission. But only on the mountain in the presence of Jesus' intimate friends did the Father ask for commitment: "Hear him" (Matthew 17:5).

The Greek word used for "hear" in this verse is not referring to either our ability to hear or even our ability to understand what we hear. It means "to yield to." We would probably use the phrase "hear and obey" to convey this thought.

In other words, to Peter, James, and John, God the Father was saying, "You have walked with my Son for three years. You have observed His miracles. You have participated in His ministry. You have heard His teachings. Now you have seen His glory. It is time to decide what you will do: Will you yield to His authority as your God?"

God still makes the same declaration to every human being: "This is my Son." Some stand on the riverbank and merely marvel at the hoopla. Others simply walk away. But a few who climb the high mountain with Jesus, actually behold His glory. To those the Father says, "Will you yield to His authority?"

American hymn writer and evangelist Judson W. Van de Venter wrote the lyrics to *I Surrender All*. His desire to yield to Jesus is clear:

All to Jesus I surrender,
Humbly at His feet I bow,
Worldly pleasures all forsaken,
Take me, Jesus, take me now.

All to Jesus I surrender,
Make me, Savior, wholly Thine.
Let me feel the Holy Spirit,
Truly know that Thou art mine.

But he also acknowledges the difficulty of surrender when he prays, "Make me, Savior, wholly Thine" and "Take me, Jesus, take me now."

Our stubborn human hearts resist God's command to yield. Our prayer must be, Take what I grasp so tightly. Pry open my clenched fist. Make me surrender all so that you can "fill me with Thy love and power." Will we be hearers or yielders? That's a choice we make every day.

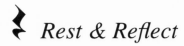 *Rest & Reflect*

James 1:22-25 explains the difference between "hearers" and "yielders." Which are you?

I LOVE BEING A PICKLE

I've known the words of Galatians 2:20 since I was in Miss Smith's fourth grade class at Lakeland Christian School. It's a tongue twister, for sure, but once you master the rhythm of its phrases, it sticks to your brain cells like the tale of Peter Piper and his peck of pickled peppers.

Understanding the theology of the verse, however, was a different matter. In fact, all those "I's" and "live's" became fairly jumbled in my gray matter. Then one day I was reading James Boice's commentary on Romans 6. In explaining the concepts of "dead to sin" but "alive to God," he used an illustration that made sense to me.

> *I am crucified with Christ: nevertheless I live; yet not I, but Christ liveth in me: and the life that I now live in the flesh I live by the faith of the Son of God, who loved me, and gave himself for me.*
> *Galatians 2:20 (KJV)*

Dr. Boice referred to a second century recipe that described the process of making pickles because the recipe used two of the same Greek words Paul used in Romans 6: The cucumbers were first dipped into boiling water [they died], and then they were immersed [made alive] in a vinegar solution. The immersion produced a permanent change in the cucumber.*

The pickle example works for Galatians 2:20 just as well as it works for Romans 6. If Paul had been talking to cucumbers instead of to the Galatians, he might have said something like this: You are no longer cucumbers. In fact, now that you have been boiled in the water and immersed in the spiced vinegar, you will never be cucumbers again. You are now pickles. Your outward appearance may seem the same, but your insides have been totally changed, permeated by the spiced vinegar. Your cucumber days are over. The spiced vinegar has produced a permanent change in you.

Now I know that sounds a bit silly, but the point of my paraphrase is accurate. Once we have been "immersed" in the precious blood of the Lamb of God, we are a new creation (2 Corinthians 5:17). We can't go back to our former state any more than a pickle can climb out of its jar and return to the vegetable garden. And even if the pickle could do that, it would not be able to re-attach itself to the cucumber vine. It would simply rot on the ground. What pickle would make that choice? And why would any Christian want to return to his former lifestyle, either?

Edwin O. Excell was a singer and songwriter who traveled with several different evangelists during the late 1800s and early 1900s. He wrote the lyrics and music of *Since I Have Been Redeemed*. In it he declared:

> *I have a song I love to sing,*
> *Since I have been redeemed*
> *Of my Redeemer, Savior, King –*
> *Since I have been redeemed.*

> *I have a Christ that satisfies,*
> *Since I have been redeemed,*
> *To do His will my highest prize –*
> *Since I have been redeemed.*

In pickle language he's saying, "No way am I going to make a run for the vegetable garden. I love being a pickle." Me too. How about you?

*James M. Boice. *Romans*. Volume 2. Grand Rapids: Baker Books, 1992, p. 659

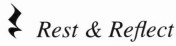 *Rest & Reflect*

*Paul lists the characteristics of "cucumbers"
and "pickles" in Colossians 3:5-17. What
"pickle" traits will you work on this week?*

OUR ETERNAL REFUGE

he lyrics for the Isaac Watts' hymn, *O God Our Help in Ages Past* are based on Psalm 90. Many biblical scholars believe that Moses wrote this psalm near the end of his life, perhaps after the trilogy of traumatic events recorded in Numbers 20 — the death of Miriam, his own disobedience at Meribah Kadesh, and the death of Aaron.

> *Lord, you have been our dwelling place throughout all generations.*
> *Before the mountains were born or you brought forth the earth and the world,*
> *from everlasting to everlasting you are God.*
> *Psalm 90:1-2 (NIV)*

Moses began his song with a declaration of God's unchanging nature. Very few things in the life of a desert dweller had permanence, and Moses had lived in the desert for 80 years. Daily he dealt with the shifting desert landscapes and the complications that arose from tent dwelling. Daily he dodged the mood swings of 2 million desert travelers.

Therefore, Moses anchored his somber reflection to the one truth that remained unmoving in his uncertain life—the everlasting, ever-faithful character of his God. Then he compared God to the one feature of his desert world that was equally immovable—the mountains.

If Moses wrote this psalm after the events of Numbers 20, his earthly sojourn was almost over. Moses died later that year, just before the Israelites crossed the Jordan and began to take possession of their inheritance. As he reviewed the 120 years of his life, three eternal truths rose up like Mount Sinai: Everything about God is permanent; everything about humans is fleeting; the only works that endure are those that bear God's stamp of approval.

Moses had triumphs like no other human being has ever had: Defeating Pharaoh, crossing the Red Sea, molding a nation of warriors out of a clump of slaves, and most significantly, communing with God face to face.

He also had sorrows that no human being ever wants to experience: In the years following the rebellion at Kadesh-Barnea, he watched an entire generation die—approximately 1.2 million people which averages out to 85 people each day, every day.* He also saw the ground swallow his cousin Korah (Numbers 16:31-33); he witnessed the Levites' execution of 3,000 rebels (Exodus 32:28); he climbed Mount Nebo and surveyed the land he would not enter before he died (Deuteronomy 34:1-4).

Nevertheless, the triumphs did not shake Moses' dependence on God, and the tragedies did not shake his confidence in the goodness of God. In his final message to Israel he proclaimed, "The eternal God is your refuge, and underneath are the everlasting arms" (Deuteronomy 33:27).

We are also desert travelers. The winds of economic uncertainty swirl about us. The shifting sands of personal health sometimes lay us flat on our backs. The blazing heat of emotional turmoil parches our souls. But like Moses and Watts we have an Eternal Refuge—God is our Shield and our Helper. He will cradle us in His everlasting arms of love so that we can continue to sing:

> *O God our help in ages past,*
> *Our hope for years to come,*
> *Our shelter from the stormy blast,*
> *And our eternal home!*
>
> *Under the shadow of Thy throne*
> *Still may we dwell secure;*
> *Sufficient is Thy arm alone,*
> *And our defense is sure.*

*Leon Wood. *A Survey of Israel's History* (revised and enlarged edition), Grand Rapids: Zondervan, 1986, p. 129.

♫ *Rest & Reflect*

Are you feeling blasted by desert wind and heat today? Read
Psalm 90 and refresh your soul by absorbing its truths.

_____

_____

_____

_____

_____

_____

_____

_____

_____

_____

_____

_____

_____

_____

_____

_____

_____

_____

_____

_____

_____

THE FINAL LECTURE

On September 18, 2007, a professor at Carnegie Mellon University delivered his last lecture. What provoked a global response was the fact that the professor, Randy Pausch, had just been diagnosed with terminal pancreatic cancer. He was dying, but his lecture focused on living— "Really Achieving Your Childhood Dreams."

Who is the Rock except our God? It is God who arms me with strength and makes my way perfect.
Psalm 18:31-32 (NIV)

Several thousand years ago, another man gave a series of last lectures. He, too, knew he would soon die. He could have used the same title Dr. Pausch did, for he also spoke about overcoming obstacles and achieving dreams. His name was Moses. We call his lectures Deuteronomy.

What I find so compelling about Deuteronomy is Moses' refusal to do what most humans do when they know they are dying: Talk about their personal accomplishments and their unfulfilled dreams. Instead

Moses directed his listeners' attention to Jehovah, the "LORD your God [who] carried you, as a father carries his son, all the way you went until you reached this place" (Deuteronomy 1:31).

In the climatic moments of Moses' final words to the Israelites, he referred to God as *tsuwr*, "the Rock," five times. Moses said in 32:3-4,

> I will proclaim the name of the LORD.
> Oh, praise the greatness of our God!
> He is the Rock, his works are perfect,
> And all his ways are just.
> A faithful God who does no wrong,
> Upright and just is he.

In these two verses, Moses emphasized four unchanging characteristics of God: Perfection, justice, faithfulness, and righteousness. Later in the chapter he spoke of "the Rock his Savior," the "Rock who fathered you," and the Rock who is unlike any other rock (vv. 15, 18, 31).

David must have loved this passage in the Pentateuch, for in seven of his psalms he calls God his Rock. He also understood that clinging to the Eternal Rock was the only way to survive the storms of life: "Who is the Rock except our God? It is God who arms me with strength and makes my way perfect"(Psalm 18:31-32).

Centuries later an English clergyman, Edward

Mote, paid tribute to the Rock. He wrote the lyrics to *The Solid Rock*:

> *My hope is built on nothing less*
> *Than Jesus' blood and righteousness;*
> *I dare not trust the sweetest frame,*
> *But wholly lean on Jesus' name.*
>
> *On Christ the solid rock I stand,*
> *All other ground is sinking sand.*
> *All other ground is sinking sand.*

Near the pulpit where Edward Mote preached for 26 years is an inscription which reads: "In loving memory of Mr. Edward Mote . . . the beloved pastor of this church, preaching Christ and Him crucified, as all the sinner can need, and all the saint desire."

In the first chapter of Professor Randy Pausch's bestseller memoir, *The Last Lecture*, he asked, "What wisdom would we impart to the world if we knew it was our last chance?"* Moses, David, and Edward Mote answered that question in unison: Cling to the Rock. Hopefully, that will be the legacy all of us who love Jesus Christ, the Solid Rock, will leave behind.

*Randy Pausch. *The Last Lecture*. New York: Hyperion, 2008.

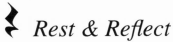 *Rest & Reflect*

What would be the theme of your "final lecture"?
Consider what the psalmist says in Psalm 71 as he looks
back on his life.

ETERNITY IN OUR HEARTS AND ON OUR DASHBOARDS

My high school friend, Velma Cloud, drove an old Chevy that her father and brothers had pieced together. It wouldn't have won any beauty contests, but it faithfully transported the members of our youth group to church activities and the local pizzeria.

Velma had attached a variety of plastic magnetic slogans on the cracked vinyl dashboard of her car. One of them displayed the familiar blue and green shapes of a world map and asked, What on earth are you doing for heaven's sake?

> *He has planted eternity in their hearts.*
> *Ecclesiastes 3:11 (NLT)*

She liked that magnet because its message reminded her that she was a member of two worlds, not just one. I remember the magnet because its message symbolized the lives of Velma and her family.

The Cloud family lived in a small wood-framed house on the outskirts of our Central Florida town. Mr.

Cloud ran a welding business in his backyard. Velma raised rabbits and decorated cakes to supplement the family income. Her family's worldly possessions were few; their spiritual riches were vast.

Their back door was constantly open to the teens at our church. I ate a lot of cookies and quite a few bowls of rabbit stew at their kitchen table. Actually, the Clouds welcomed everyone into their home with an invitation "to sit down and visit a while." Mrs. Cloud always asked, "Can I get you a glass of tea?"

The Clouds were support beams in our fifty-family church. Mrs. Cloud rocked babies and wiped noses in the nursery—every Sunday. Mr. Cloud greeted folks and passed out bulletins—every Sunday.

The Cloud family consistently modeled the art of living on earth with a clear view of heaven. They had plenty of difficulties—financially and physically—but every Wednesday night at prayer meeting they thanked the Lord for all their blessings. On Sunday nights they sang *When We All Get to Heaven* with contagious gusto from the third pew on the right.

That kind of double vision is essential for Christians— seeing everything on earth alongside all that awaits us in heaven. That's one of the reasons songs about heaven stir our souls. We long for the day when we will join the angel choirs around the throne of God, singing "Holy, holy, holy" (Revelation 4:6-11). We long for the life John describes in Revelation 21:4—when "there will be no more death or mourning or crying or pain."

When heaven becomes the permanent desktop background on the monitors of our lives, the circumstantial icons that clutter our days and steal our sleep at night lose

92

their power over us. Then we begin to walk confidently with the spiritual double vision that kept the Cloud family on a steady course, and we can sing Eliza Hewitt's lyrics with genuine gusto:

> *Let us then be true and faithful,*
> *Trusting, serving every day;*
> *Just one glimpse of Him in glory*
> *Will the toils of life repay.*

> *When we all get to heaven*
> *What a day of rejoicing that will be!*
> *When we all see Jesus,*
> *We'll sing and shout the victory!*

And others will remember our joyful love for Jesus long after the song has ended.

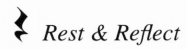 *Rest & Reflect*

Read Revelation 21:1-4 and 22:1-5.
What aspects of your future life in heaven fill your heart with joy?

PALM SUNDAY —A BITTERSWEET DAY

erhaps on that bittersweet day Jesus slipped out of Mary and Martha's home early in the morning and found a solitary place to commune with his Father (Mark 1:35). He did rise early enough to send two of his disciples into a nearby village to borrow a donkey (Luke 19:29-30). While they were gone, the people who had feasted with Jesus the previous evening gathered at the home of his Bethany friends and traveled with him into Jerusalem (John 12:12).

Because of the exuberant crowd, we often refer to this occasion as "the triumphal entry"; however, Jesus viewed it from a different perspective. It was the tenth day of the Feast of Passover—the day each Jewish family selected an unblemished lamb, brought it into their homes, and set it apart for the atonement of their sins. On this day, the Lamb of God entered Jerusalem, presenting himself as

> *Hosanna! Blessed is he who comes in the name of the Lord.*
> *Mark 11:9 (NIV)*

the perfect, once-for-all sacrifice that would atone for the sins of every human being.

Luke alone tells us that as the entourage reached the crest of the hill that led down into Jerusalem, Jesus began to weep. Mourning the rejection of the people he had come to redeem Jesus said, "If you, even you, had only known on this day what would bring you peace—but now it is hidden from your eyes" (Luke 19:42).

Maybe he smiled and greeted the people who fell in behind his disciples and joined their anthem of praises. Maybe the sorrow in his soul lingered in his eyes even as the *hosannas* rained down on him like confetti.

Jesus knew what lay ahead. He knew the cheers would dissolve into jeers and that some of the people waving palm branches would soon be clenching their fists. He knew that some *hosannas* would change to shrieks of "crucify him."

Nevertheless, Jesus loved the people who stood along the roadside anyway, and he allowed them the honor of proclaiming the truth: He was the Son of David. He was the King. He was the Messiah. But he was not merely a prophet as some of them declared (Matthew 21:11). He was God Incarnate, who had chosen to come to earth as their Redeemer.

We also proclaim Jesus' true identity when we sing hymns like *All Glory, Laud, and Honor* on Palm Sunday:

All glory, laud, and honor
To Thee, Redeemer, King,
To whom the lips of children
Made sweet hosannas ring:
Thou art the King of Israel,
Thou David's royal Son,
Who in the Lord's name comest,
The King and blessed one!

But our "hymns of praise" should be seasoned with the bittersweet truth that not all who shout *hosanna* bow before Jesus as Lord and Savior.

As we follow Jesus through the week of His passion, let us not forget the sorrow that accompanied our Savior every step of the way. And let us not forfeit what so many in the cheering crowds renounced that week: The peace *with* God that Jesus' atonement provided and the peace *of* God that He longs for us to enjoy every day of our lives.

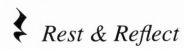 *Rest & Reflect*

What can you do today to honor Jesus as
"The King and blessed one"?
Consider what Jesus asked Peter to do in John 21:15-22.

How Do I "Survey" the Cross?

Three hundred years before Mel Gibson decided to remind people of the suffering Jesus endured on the cross, Isaac Watts wrote the lyrics of *When I Survey the Wondrous Cross*. The third stanza, in particular, graphically portrays the cost of the Cross:

> *See, from His head, His hands, His feet,*
> *Sorrow and love flow mingled down:*
> *Did e'er such love and sorrow meet,*
> *Or thorns compose so rich a crown?*

The poignancy of the phrase "sorrow and love flow mingled down" is echoed in the fourth stanza, which is omitted in most American hymnals: "His dying crimson, like a robe, Spreads o'er His body on the tree." These images, simultaneously beautiful and horrific, have brought tears

But whatever was to my profit I now consider loss for the sake of Christ. Philippians 3:7

99

to the eyes of devout Christians for centuries. However, stirring our emotions was not Watts' primary purpose for composing this beloved hymn.

Watts revealed his intent in the final stanza: "Love so amazing, so divine, Demands my soul, my life, my all." In another of his hymns, *Alas, and Did My Savior Bleed*, Watts communicates a similar thought: "But drops of grief can ne'er repay the debt of love I owe: Here, Lord, I give myself away— 'Tis all that I can do."

God never intended for us to simply cry over Christ's suffering. Gibson's movie prompted thousands of people to weep over the agony Jesus endured, yet they still walked out of the theaters without acknowledging Him as Savior and Lord.

Unfortunately, my response to Christ's suffering is sometimes more like the movie theatre crowd's than I like to admit. I come to the Lord's Communion Table with too much emotion and not enough humility. I am moved but not changed, sorrowful but not repentant. If Jesus' sacrifice does not drive me to repentance and obedience, then it has not truly affected me, no matter how many tears I shed.

The verb "survey" means "to view in detail," but Watts had more than careful observation in mind when he encouraged Christians to survey the "cross on which the Prince of Glory died." When we truly survey the cross, kneeling in awe before the astounding love that was poured out for us there, it alters the way we live. Paul said, "I consider everything a loss compared to the surpassing greatness of knowing Christ Jesus my Lord" (Philippians 3:8). Watts wrote, "all the vain things that charm me most, I sacrifice them to His blood."

Therefore, singing *When I Survey the Wondrous Cross* and participating in communion should be more than a time of remembrance and tears. These acts of worship should prune our souls and motivate us to act upon the words we sing:

> *My richest gain I count but loss,*
> *And pour contempt on all my pride.*

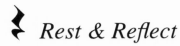 *Rest & Reflect*

Read Philippians 3:3-12.
What kinds of things did Paul "consider loss"?
What did he value? What do you value most?

BEYOND DESCRIPTION

My husband Mace opened the back door and hollered, "Hon, come and see this." Since I was chopping vegetables for dinner I answered, "I'll be there in a minute."

"You'd better hurry," he urged.

Mace often calls for me when he is working in the yard. He wants me to see the bush he has transplanted, the fence he has mended, or the brush he has cleared. But when he adds, "hurry," it's usually because one of our cats is doing something that will amuse me.

> *God has raised this Jesus to life, and we are all witnesses of the fact.*
> *Acts 2:32 (NIV)*

So I rinsed my hands and headed outside. Mace was standing in the middle of our street, and he motioned for me to join him. As I approached, he pointed to the end of our cul de sac. Arching over the end of our street was a brilliant double rainbow. We marveled over the vivid colors and the completeness of the bow. In a few moments, the clouds shifted and the angle of

103

the sunlight changed. The rainbow faded.

If I had waited, I would have missed it. And no description could have evoked the wonder of witnessing that fleeting display of God's artistry. Sometimes words just cannot capture the beauty of nature, the joy of an occasion, or the marvel of a discovery. You simply must experience it yourself.

On Easter morning, a group of women approached the tomb where Jesus' body lay. There they were greeted by an angel who assured them, "He is not here; he has risen, just as he said. Come and see the place where he lay" (Matthew 28:6).

No words could convey the marvel of that moment. When the women returned to the disciples, they tried to explain what had occurred at the tomb. However, the men "did not believe the women, because their words seemed . . . like nonsense" (Luke 24:11). Later, Peter and John did go to the tomb. When they saw, they too believed (John 20:8). The experience erased their doubts.

Thomas Kelley, an Anglican priest, wrote the lyrics to *Come, See the Place Where Jesus Lay*. In it he said, "Now let our songs His triumph tell, Who burst the bands of death and hell." But he also added:

> *Ye ransomed, let your praise resound,*
> *And in your Master's work abound,*
> *Steadfast, immovable;*
> *Be sure your labor's not in vain;*

Kelley recognized that the most effective witness of Jesus' power to transform lives is not the words we speak or the songs we sing—it is what people see with their own eyes. As people see the Master's work abounding in our lives, their doubts dissipate. Instead of saying "listen to me" we can say, "Come and see. Come and see what God is doing in my life, in my family, in my church." Who knows what the result of such an openhearted invitation will be?

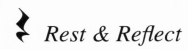

Rest & Reflect

Do people see the Master's work abounding in your life?
Consider what Peter said in 1 Peter 2:11-17.

A SHELTER
IN A WEARY LAND

*I*n the little church I attended as a child, we sang a lot of gospel songs on Sunday nights. One of the congregation's favorites was *A Shelter in the Time of Storm*. The chorus' first line puzzled me: "O Jesus is a rock in a weary land." I wondered how land could be tired.

Vernon Charlesworth based the lyrics for his song on Isaiah 32:1-2. Although the passage refers to a human king and the citizens of his realm, Charlesworth applied the descriptions to Jesus. He is our refuge — "a shelter from the wind" and our sustainer — "a stream in the desert." He is our protector — "the shadow of a great rock in a weary land."

> *The Lord is my rock, my fortress and my deliverer;*
> *my God is my rock, in whom I take refuge.*
> *Psalm 18:2 (NIV)*

The Hebrew word sometimes translated "weary" means "parched" or "thirsty." It often referred to

107

someone who was worn out from traveling or working. David used the word in Psalm 143 when he prayed for God's deliverance from a difficult situation: "I spread out my hands to you; my soul thirsts for you like a parched land" (v.6).

We all become parched sometimes. We face adversaries that seem unbeatable and pray about situations that seem unsolvable. The desert road we travel seems endless. In fact, we feel like Hannah did in 1 Samuel 1. Hannah's soul-crushing burden was her inability to have children. Her husband's solution was a second wife, Peninnah, who did have a fruitful womb. That gave Elkanah heirs, but it only increased Hannah's misery because Peninnah taunted Hannah mercilessly.

In 1 Samuel 1, Hannah poured out her soul to Jehovah. God graciously responded and she gave birth to Samuel. Chapter 2 records Hannah's prayer of praise. In it, she focused on three attributes of God that sustained her through years of sorrow and suffering— His holiness, His power, and His protection:

> My heart rejoices in the LORD;
> In the LORD my horn is lifted high,
> My mouth boasts over my enemies,
> For I delight in your deliverance.
> There is no one holy like the LORD;
> There is no one besides you;
> There is no Rock like you (vv. 1-2).

By praising God's holiness, Hannah acknowledged that everything God does is right. He never makes mistakes. By praising His power (horn), she recognized that God alone was able to solve her problem. By using Moses' name for God, the Rock, she affirmed that God had remained faithful to her throughout her ordeal.

As Hannah and her family traveled to Shiloh each year to offer sacrifices, they would have passed through the rocky hill country of Ephraim. Perhaps they found refuge from a storm or from the sun beneath a massive boulder—and the protection of that stone canopy reminded her of Jehovah.

We, too, can find refuge and refreshment beneath the Rock of our Salvation when we journey through weary lands. As Charlesworth wrote:

> *The Lord's our rock, in Him we hide,*
> *A shelter in the time of storm;*
> *Secure whatever ill betide,*
> *A shelter in the time of storm.*
>
> *A shade by day, defense by night,*
> *A shelter in the time of storm;*
> *No fears alarm, no fears affright,*
> *A shelter in the time of storm.*

♩ *Rest & Reflect*

Read Hannah's prayer in 1 Samuel 2:1-10. What does she include in her list of praises? What's on your list?

THE BEAUTY OF HOLINESS—HIS AND OURS

Many verses in the Bible convict me. Some, like Leviticus 19:2, sound downright intimidating: "Be holy, because I, the Lord your God, am holy." In my head, I know that personal holiness is possible as I allow the Holy Spirit to purify my heart and mind. Still the word *holy* makes me uncomfortable because I also know my heart is not completely set apart to God on a daily basis. Consequently, I spend a lot more time praising God for His mercy and His grace than for His holiness.

Give unto the LORD the glory due unto his name; worship the LORD in the beauty of holiness.
Psalm 29:2 (KJV)

Nevertheless, several Bible passages refer to the beauty of God's holiness. I don't normally pair those two nouns, but God does. And as I studied the context of these verses, the Holy Spirit began to change my attitude about holiness.

111

Three psalms mention the *beauty* (KJV) or *splendor* (NIV) of holiness. David wrote Psalm 29 after he witnessed a fierce storm which inspired him to praise the superior majesty of the storm's Creator: "Give unto the LORD the glory due unto his name; worship the LORD in the beauty of holiness" (v. 2 KJV).

When David was transporting the Ark of the Covenant to Jerusalem, he wrote Psalm 96 to honor the occasion. In gratitude for God's numerous blessings, the people sang, "Ascribe to the LORD the glory due his name; Worship the LORD in the splendor of his holiness" (vv. 8-9). In both Psalm 29 and 96 David linked God's mighty acts and awesome power to His holiness. In other words, he recognized that God's actions are manifestations of His holiness.

Psalm 110 also connects beauty to holiness. This psalm describes Jesus' future reign. But in verse three, the phrase "in beauties of holiness" (KJV) describes God's people, not God himself. The NIV says, "Your troops will be . . . arrayed in holy majesty."

How can sinful humans be clothed in "holy majesty"? Hebrews 10:10 states, "we have been made holy through the sacrifice of the body of Jesus Christ once for all." God declares that we are holy because He always looks at us through the purifying, redemptive work of our Savior, Jesus Christ.

Therefore, God's holiness shouldn't frighten us; it should fill our hearts with gratitude. God the Father demonstrated His holy power when he chose to redeem us. Jesus' holy sacrifice on the Cross purified us. The Holy Spirit enables us to reflect God's holiness in our daily lives.

Someday we will be physically clothed in the beauty of God's holiness, "dressed in fine linen, white and clean" (Revelation 19:14). We will join the angel choirs as they praise God's holiness "day and night" (Revelation 4:8). Ignaz Franz described that scene in *Holy God, We Praise Thy Name*:

> *Hark, the glad celestial hymn*
> *Angel choirs above are raising;*
> *Cherubim and seraphim,*
> *In unceasing chorus praising;*
> *Fill the heavens with sweet accord:*
> *Holy, holy, holy Lord.*
>
> *Holy God we praise Thy name;*
> *Lord of all, we bow before Thee;*
> *All on earth Thy scepter claim,*
> *All in heaven above adore Thee:*
> *Infinite Thy vast domain,*
> *Everlasting is Thy reign.*

Forever rejoicing in His radiant presence, forever reflecting His purity and goodness—that's the beauty of holiness.

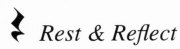

Rest & Reflect

What does holiness look like in our daily lives?
Read Peter's explanation in
1 Peter 1:13-16 and 2:9.

THE POWER OF JESUS' NAME

When I was a child, one of my favorite Bible stories was the healing of the paralytic man in Mark 2. The idea of four men tearing apart someone's roof to get their friend to Jesus delighted me.

> *Salvation is found in no one else, for there is no other name under heaven given to men by which we must be saved.*
> *Acts 4:12 (NIV)*

I didn't understand why Jesus didn't punish them for that, but I certainly admired their fearless ingenuity!

I still smile when I read that story, but what intrigues me now is Jesus' conversation with the religious leaders who were present. They were offended by Jesus' statement, "Son, your sins are forgiven." They thought, *He's blaspheming. Who can forgive sins but God alone?*

They assumed that Jesus was just a charlatan who claimed to have God's power. Jesus confronted them immediately asking, "Why are you thinking these things?"

115

He then healed the paralytic's body as a demonstration of His authority to forgive sins. The religious leaders, along with the rest of the crowd, were amazed. They praised God and said, "We have never seen anything like this!" (Mark 2:12)

How disappointed Jesus must have been! It was so human to be mesmerized by the physical healing and completely unmoved by the spiritual healing that had just occurred. Unfortunately, many of us are just like that crowd—we evaluate the potency of God's power by what we can see. Does He heal our loved ones? Does He provide the jobs we need? Does He protect us from injury in car accidents?

What we fail to remember is that these physical signs of His power would be meaningless from an eternal perspective if Jesus could not forgive sins. Jesus said it Himself in John 17:2, "Father, the time has come. Glorify your Son, that your Son may glorify you. For you have given him authority [*power*, KJV] over all people that he might give eternal life to all those you have given him." The most awesome manifestation of Jesus' power is His ability to transform unholy sinners into immortal beings that can live forever in God's presence.

Edward Perronet's hymn, *All Hail the Power of Jesus' Nam*e, looks forward to the day when people from every nation will join the angelic choirs as they praise God:

> *All hail the power of Jesus' name!*
> *Let angels prostrate fall,*
> *Bring forth the royal diadem,*
> *And crown him Lord of all!*

116

The hymn also refers to Philippians 2:10 which states, "At the name of Jesus every knee shall bow and every tongue confess that Jesus Christ is Lord":

> *Let every kindred, every tribe,*
> *On this terrestrial ball,*
> *To Him all majesty ascribe,*
> *And crown Him Lord of all!*

Every creature on earth and in heaven will bow before Jesus Christ not because He has the power to heal the lame but because He has the power to forgive sins. Let's avoid the mistake the crowd in Mark 2 made. Let's look beyond the temporary evidence of Jesus' power in our lives and sing our loudest praises to the One who forgives our sins:

> *Hail Him who saves you by His grace*
> *And crown Him Lord of all.*

 *Rest & Reflect*

What did Jesus say to the disciples about power and
authority in Mark 10:42-43?
How does that apply to us?

OUR TRANSCENDENT GOD

illiam Williams wrote hundreds of hymns. Only one of them, *Guide Me, O Thou Great Jehovah* is consistently included in American hymnals. Williams wrote these lyrics in 1745 during the early years of the Welsh Methodist revival. And although Williams was also a renowned Welsh preacher, his hymn lyrics are his true legacy.

> **The Lord himself goes before you and will be with you; he will never leave you nor forsake you. Do not be afraid; do not be discouraged.**
> **Deuteronomy 31:8 (NIV)**

Guide Me, O Thou Great Jehovah originally had five stanzas. Each stanza balances the solidity of God's character with the feebleness of humanity. Williams contrasts God's power with our weakness, His steadfastness with our doubt, His triumphs with our failures.

In the first two stanzas, he draws us back to the wilderness journey of the Israelites. Perhaps Williams

119

had been studying Deuteronomy 8 when he wrote his hymn. Like Moses, he refers to the mighty power of God displayed at the Red Sea, the provision of manna, and the water from the rock. Like Moses, he also emphasizes that God's blessings should motivate His people to both obey Him and praise Him (8:10-20).

In the third stanza, Williams connects God's mighty acts in the Old Testament to the matchless power He displayed at the cross when He conquered "Sin, and Satan, and the grave." Then he shifts from our present journey through a "barren land" to the glorious future that awaits us. He reminds us that God will lead us safely through death and into heaven: "Land me safe on Canaan's side."

The fifth stanza, omitted in many American hymnals, also focuses on the future:

> *Musing on my habitation,*
> *Musing on my heav'nly home,*
> *Fills my soul with holy longings:*
> *Come, my Jesus, quickly come;*
> *Vanity is all I see;*
> *Lord, I long to be with Thee!*
> *Lord, I long to be with Thee!*

The wistful tone of this final stanza suggests Williams might have grown weary of the discord between the Armenian and Calvinist factions of his era. It's as if he were saying, "We have a majestic God. As His people, we have spectacular history. We have received a magnificent salvation, and we look forward to a glorious

120

future. So many reasons to rejoice — why are we arguing about these other matters?"

The writer of Hebrews also reflected on the history and blessings of God's people. He concluded, "Therefore, since we are surrounded by such a great cloud of witnesses, let us throw aside everything that hinders and the sin that so easily entangles, and . . . let us fix our eyes on Jesus" (Hebrews 12:1-2).

So much in our daily lives seeks to pull us down and under. In *Guide Me O Thou Great Jehovah*, William lifts our gaze to our Transcendent God, our Strong Deliverer. He will lead us safely through all earthly deserts and difficulties if we "fix our eyes on Jesus."

♪ *Rest & Reflect*

Are your eyes fixed on our transcendent God today? Read Deuteronomy 8:10-20 and then meditate on all the ways God has been good to you.

HUMBLE BOLDNESS AT THE THRONE OF GRACE

ne of the most memorable phrases in English literature belongs to Charles Dickens' Oliver Twist: "Please, sir, can I have some more?" Oliver's bold request for more food enraged the workhouse master, but it won the admiration of his peers and in that moment a classic literary hero was born.

> *Let us then approach the throne of grace with confidence, so that we may receive mercy and find grace to help us in our time of need.*
> *Hebrews 4:16 (NIV)*

The writer of Psalm 5 displayed a similar mixture of humility and boldness when he prayed, "Give ear to my words, O LORD, consider my sighing. Listen to my cry for help, my King and my God, for to you I pray."

In these two verses, the psalmist described his prayer with three different nouns: He first used "words" and then "sighing" which can also be translated "groans." In verse 2, he used "cry for help"—a fervent shout. Read the phrases aloud, slowly, and you can sense the severity of this person's need.

Yet the psalmist did not sink into despair. His confidence is evident in the next verse: "I lay my requests before you and wait in expectation." He was distraught but still hopeful.

His urgent boldness reminds me of the Greek woman in Mark 7 who came to Jesus and asked him to heal her daughter who was demon-possessed. When Jesus told her that it was "not right to take the children's bread and toss it to their dogs," she requested "crumbs." And Jesus rewarded her persistence (vv. 24-30).

The tax collector who prayed, "Have mercy on me, a sinner" and the blind man who "shouted all the more" also appealed to Jesus with boldness (Luke 18:13, 39). Both times Jesus commended their faith and answered their requests. In Mark 5, the woman who touched the hem of Jesus' robe did not speak a word, but her bold act of faith pleased Jesus. He said, "Daughter, your faith has healed you. Go in peace and be freed from your suffering" (v. 34).

William Walford, a blind English preacher and writer, wrote the lyrics to *Sweet Hour of Prayer*. In it, he also reminds us that God wants to reward our confidence in His power and His goodness by answering our prayers:

> *Sweet hour of prayer, sweet hour of prayer,*
> *Thy wings shall my petition bear*
> *To Him whose truth and faithfulness*
> *Engage the waiting soul to bless:*
> *And since He bids me seek His face,*
> *Believe His Word, and trust His grace,*
> *I'll cast on Him my every care,*
> *And wait for thee, sweet hour of prayer.*

When our prayers reflect our reliance on God's promises and His truth, He reaches out to us just as He responded to people in the Bible. As the psalmist said, God spreads His protection over us, gathering us under His wings and erecting the fence of His favor around us (Psalm 5:11-12).

Oliver Twist eventually received more than he ever imagined could exist outside the workhouse walls. His grandfather filled the boy's world with love and security—a happily-ever-after tale worthy of Walt Disney. As children of God, we too will receive exceedingly, abundantly more than we could ever ask or imagine (Ephesians 3:20). And like the psalmist, we will "ever sing for joy" because we have a King who hears and heeds our cry (Psalm 5:11). Be bold. Ask for more.

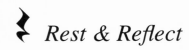 *Rest & Reflect*

Make a list of bold requests to present to the Lord, but be mindful of the warning given in James 4:2-3.

THE CHALLENGER DEEP

*S*cientists claim that the deepest point of the earth's oceans is the Challenger Deep found within The Marianas Trench, which is a deep crack in the floor of the western Pacific Ocean. The trench's bottom is 36,200 feet below sea level—almost 7 miles. By comparison, a stack of 28 Empire State Buildings would measure 35,000 feet or 6.6 miles. Personally, I cannot wrap my imagination around those kinds of numbers, but Romans 8:39 tells me that even if I could fathom that kind of depth, God's love for me is deeper still.

> *Neither height nor depth nor anything else in all creation will be able to separate us from the love of God that is in Christ Jesus.*
> *Romans 8:39 (NIV)*

A long time ago, a Hebrew prophet named Jonah tried to distance himself from God. He tried the width of the ocean first. When that didn't work, he endured the depths of the ocean for three days before he finally realized that nothing was going to prohibit God's tough love from reaching him.

127

Centuries later, Samuel Trevor Francis tried to escape God's love in the dismal depths of London. One night, alone and despairing, he considered throwing himself into the murky waters of the Thames River. He testified afterward that God prevented him from jumping off the Hungersford Bridge and that the experience inspired him to write *O the Deep, Deep Love of Jesus*.*

King David once asked, "Where can I go from your Spirit? Where can I flee from your presence?" (Psalm 139:7). The answer of course is "nowhere." David said, "If I rise on the wings of the dawn, if I settle on the far side of the sea, even there your hand will guide me, your right hand will hold me fast" (139:9-10). God's inescapable love filled David's heart with devotion. He longed to be even closer to His God (139:23-24).

Whether we discover the depths of God's love by pushing against its boundaries as Jonah did or by wrapping ourselves in its warmth as David did, we ultimately learn that nothing can separate us from the God who loves us with an everlasting love (Jeremiah 31:3).

Paul told the Ephesians that exploring the borderlands of God's love was part of spiritual maturation. In fact, his prayer for the Ephesians was "that you, being rooted and established in love, may have power, together with all the saints, to grasp how wide and long and high and deep is the love of Christ" (3:17-18).

Jesus' love for us propelled Him from the glistening heights of heaven to the sunless abyss of death. The width of His love stretches to every human being. No scientific gizmo will ever be able to affix a number to its dimensions.

> *O the deep, deep love of Jesus*
> *Vast, unmeasured, boundless, free!*
> *Rolling as a mighty ocean*
> *In its fullness over me*
> *Underneath me, all around me,*
> *Is the current of Thy love —*
> *It lifts me up to glory,*
> *For it lifts me up to Thee.*

*For more of Francis story, go to the Center for Church Music website: http://www.songsandhymns.org.

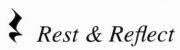 *Rest & Reflect*

*Are you exploring the borderlands of God's love? Read
Psalm 136 and then write down a few examples from your
own life that prove "His love endures forever."*

CAUGHT IN A DOWNPOUR?

My pastor gives our congregation glimpses of his spiritual journey in a weekly email. In one letter he focused on "fighting for joy," and part of his strategy for waging this spiritual battle was "giving himself a good talking to." I understood exactly what he meant.

When a thunderstorm of adversity rains down on us, it's difficult to maintain a sunny countenance. Even with the umbrella of Truth over our heads, we can still get drenched. And then, if you're like me, your faith gets a little soggy and limp. Psalms 42 and 43 describe the emotional state of someone who felt that way. In essence, the psalmist is giving himself, and everyone who reads or sings the psalms, a "good talking to."

> *We wait in hope for the LORD; he is our help and our shield.*
> *In him our hearts rejoice, for we trust in his holy name.*
> *Psalm 33:20-21 (NIV)*

Three times in these two psalms the speaker asks, "Why are you downcast, O my soul? Why are you so disturbed within me?" The Hebrew word translated *downcast* basically means "thrown down to the ground." Isaiah described it this way:

> Brought low, you will speak from the ground;
> Your speech will mumble out of the dust,
> Your voice will come ghostlike from the earth;
> Out of the dust your speech will whisper. (29:4)

The Hebrew word translated *disturbed* refers to the mournful moans of someone who is caught in a snare — think of a trapped animal's cries of pain. Together, the two Hebrew words portray someone writhing in agony, helpless and alone.

The psalmist lists several reasons for his distress. He is far from home (vv. 2, 4); enemies mock his faith (v. 3, 10); he thinks God has abandoned him (42:9; 43:2). However, as he gives himself "a good talking to," he focuses on what he knows to be true about God. God is His Rock (42:9). God is His Savior (42:11; 43:5). God is His stronghold (43:2). God sends forth His light and His truth as a rescue squad (43:2). Three times the speaker identifies the correct solution for his dilemma: "Put your hope in God." Hope is his deliverer.

Biblical hope is not a foolish indulgence in wishful thinking — it is unshakeable confidence in God's character. That's the reason both Psalm 42 and 43 end with the same phrase: "I will yet praise him, my savior and my God."

Jean Sophia Pigott wrote the lyrics to *Jesus, I Am Resting, Resting*. Little is known about this 19th century

132

Irish woman except that her poetry manifested her unwavering hope in God:

> ***Simply trusting Thee, Lord Jesus***
> ***I behold Thee as Thou art,***
> ***And Thy love, so pure, so changeless***
> ***Satisfies my heart—***
> ***Satisfies its deepest longings,***
> ***Meets, supplies its every need,***
> ***And surrounds me with its blessings:***
> ***Thine is love indeed!***

Sooner or later, we all get caught in a downpour of difficulty. But if we huddle under the umbrella of God's Word and rest in the truth it proclaims, we can still sing:

> ***Ever lift Thy face upon me***
> ***As I work and wait for Thee;***
> ***Resting 'neath Thy smile, Lord Jesus,***
> ***Earth's dark shadows flee.***
> ***Brightness of my Father's glory,***
> ***Sunshine of my Father's face,***
> ***Keeps me ever trusting, resting,***
> ***Fill me with Thy grace.***

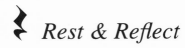

Rest & Reflect

Is your faith a little soggy and limp?
Fortify it by meditating on Psalms 42 and 43.

Song Reference Index

A Shelter in the Time of Storm......................109

All Glory, Laud and Honor 97

All Hail the Power of Jesus' Name 116

Amazing Grace..20

Blessed Be the Name......................................69

Come, See the Place Where Jesus Lay...........104

God So Loved the World.................................29

Great God, We Sing Your Mighty Hand 17

Guide Me, O Thou Great Jehovah.................120

Holy God, We Praise Thy Name 113

I Am His and He Is Mine 73

Immortal, Invisible 25

I Must Tell Jesus...56

I Surrender All...77

It Is Well with My Soul 37

Jesus, I Am Resting, Resting.........................133

O Come, O Come Emmanuel..........................45

O God, Our Help in Ages Past 85

O the Deep, Deep Love of Jesus 129

O Worship the King..49

Savior, Like a Shepherd Lead Us....................33

Since I Have Been Redeemed 81

Sing Praise to God Who Reigns Above 65

Softly and Tenderly 60

Sweet Hour of Prayer 125

The Solid Rock..89

We Sing the Greatness of Our God 53

What Child Is This?..40

When I Survey the Wondrous Cross 99

When We All Get to Heaven 93

More Inspirational Books From
❀ **Christian Devotions Books** ❀

http://www.christiandevotionsbooks.com/

Answering the Call -
Inspirational Devotionals from a Tested Paramedic
by Pat Patterson   *Price: $9.95*

Jesus said, "Greater love has no one than this, that he lay down his life for his friends." The First Responders in your community do just that. They sacrifice comfort and safety to protect the lives of others, always waiting, and always wondering when they will find themselves answering the next call. This book was written for them, but it applies to anyone who searches for courage and hope, struggles with a difficult relationship, or suffers through pain or loss. Are you seeking a closer walk with God? Wondering what comes next? Answering the Call can help you find your way. It reveals the simple truth that Jesus Christ is Lord, and that to follow him is to find true meaning in life. Christ... the First Responder, is calling you now.

Will you be answering the call? "The promise is for you and your children and for all who are far off -for all whom the Lord our God will call." - Acts 2:39.

Learn more about this book at: www.answeringthecall.us

Faith & FINANCES:
In God We Trust, A Journey to Financial Dependence
by Christian Devotions contributors   *Price: $9.95*

Jesus spoke about money and material possessions more than he talked about heaven, hell, or prayer. He noted the relationship between a man's heart and his wallet, warning, "Where your treasure is, there your heart will be." This contemporary retelling of the Rich Young Ruler brings a fresh look at the relationship between a person's faith and their finances. Within the pages of Faith & FINANCES: In God We Trust you'll find spiritual insight and practical advice from Christy award-winning writer Ann Tatlock, plus best-selling authors, Loree Lough, Yvonne Lehman, Virginia Smith, Irene Brand, DiAnn Mills, Miralee Ferrell, Shelby Rawson and many more.

Great faith calls us to trust God, not our wealth. Read how others have cast off the golden handcuffs and learned to live the abundant life Jesus promised in this contemporary retelling of the Rich Young Ruler. Faith & FINANCES: In God We Trust, A Journey to Financial Dependence - turning the hearts of a nation back toward God one paycheck at a time.

Learn more about this book at: www.faithandfinances.us

Spirit & HEART: A Devotional Journey
by Christian Devotions contributors   Price: $9.95

What is a devotional journey? It is the Bible. Today we enjoy the benefit of the prayers, wisdom, praise and sorrow of people who, during their lifetime, chose to remember the times God worked in their lives. That is devotion to God and dedication to recording "His Story." The daily devotions included in this book are heartfelt stories, lessons, and advice from others who have traveled the devotional journey. This book is a primer, a tool to get you started on the path toward spending your best moments with the Father. Christ says, where your heart is there your treasure will be. Treasure His words and whispers as you walk in the footsteps of award-winning authors Ann Tatlock, Loree Lough, Yvonne Lehman, Virginia Smith, Irene Brand, Shelby Rawson, Eddie Jones, Cindy Sproles, Ariel Allison-plus many more.

Learn more about this book at: www.devotionsbook.com

Emerson The Magnificent!
by Dwight Ritter   Price: $12.99

"A charming little book for young and old."

How an old bike takes a young man for the ride of his life.

"What a delight... though I thought it unlikely that a bicycle could do much to unravel some complicated issues, my skepticism was outvoted. It really doesn't matter how old you are, Emerson talks to you. Dwight Ritter's illustrations made me smile as much as his story warmed my heart. Emerson's message challenged my thinking, then threw me a lifeline, reeled me in and rescued me. Get it! Read it! Give it to everyone you know! " - by Pat Lindquist.

Learn more about this book at: www.emersonthemagnificent.com

**More Inspirational Books Available From
Christian Devotions Ministry's Book Division
www.christiandevotionsbooks.com**

Printed in Great Britain
by Amazon.co.uk, Ltd.,
Marston Gate.